# Angels in Disguise

A Story of Change, Loss and New Beginnings

Lawrence Balleine

Parson's Porch Books

*Angels in Disguise: A Story of Change, Loss and New Beginnings*
ISBN: Softcover 978-1-951472-78-8
Copyright © 2020 by Lawrence Balleine

All rights reserved. No part of this book may be reproduced or transmitted in any form or by any means, electronic or mechanical, including photocopying, recording, or by any information storage and retrieval system, without permission in writing from the publisher.

www.parsonsporch.com

*Angels in Disguise*

# Introduction

*Angels in Disguise* is part 3 of a series that traces the sabbatical journey of Michael Lattimore. As in the past two volumes, Michael, the chief character in all three of the books, continues his travel to the dairy farming regions of Wisconsin. A middle school social studies teacher, Michael is seeking to determine how the changes in culture are affecting the family farm. Along the way, he meets numerous people facing a variety of circumstances. These lead Michael into interactions that he never could have foreseen prior to his departure. Whereas *Entertaining Angels* is a story of change, loss and healing, and *An Angel Among Us* is a tale of change, brokenness and reconciliation, *Angels In Disguise* is a story of change, loss and new beginnings.

# Tuesday Night

"Something sure smells good. I'm guessing steak and grilled onions," said Michael as he got out of his pickup truck at the Riverview Motel. He was a few miles south of Lacrosse. It was just after 7:30 P.M. when he arrived. He hadn't eaten anything substantial since before the funeral he had attended back in Platteville. And that was several hours ago. So, after checking into the Riverview, Michael followed his nose which took him next door to the Riverview Bar and Grill.

He savored the thought of a grilled hamburger. Michael knew from experience that although "bar food" was not always the healthiest, it was almost always the tastiest. Tonight, he was opting for tasty. And then he planned to wash down the burger with a beer; not just any beer, but either a bottle or a draft of Old Style.

Why Old Style? Because even though Michael seldom drank beer, he knew Old Style was brewed in Lacrosse and he said to himself: "When in Rome...."

As he entered the establishment he immediately noticed the U-shaped bar on the west side of the large room that also contained about a dozen tables. Each could accommodate four patrons. Only one table had customers – two middle aged couples dressed in casual attire. They were playing cards. Michael assumed it was their post-dinner ritual. Michael saw that the bar was designed in such a way that all those seated at it could look out a large picture window that afforded a panoramic view of the river – the mighty Mississippi. Only two of the fifteen or sixteen bar stools were occupied. The walls were decked out in typical rural Wisconsin fare: mounts of deer, coyotes and peasants, and several species of game fish including northern pike, walleyes and bass. Among the wildlife displays were plenty of Green Bay Packers "treasures" including a vintage jersey worn by the late great linebacker Ray Nitschke and a helmet signed by Brett Favre.

Michael walked to the bar and took a seat. Immediately his eyes were drawn to the picture window and to the river beyond. It was just before 8 P.M. Nevertheless, it was still quite bright outside since the summer solstice had occurred just over a week earlier.

"What can I get for you?" asked the barkeeper.

"I'll take an Old Style, and can I also have a burger – with everything, especially grilled onions?"

"Well, I can get you that burger and an Old Style, but you might want to know that Old Style isn't brewed in Lacrosse anymore."

"I didn't know. I remember how their commercials would always end with a spokesperson saying: 'G. Heileman Brewing Company, Lacrosse, Wisconsin.' But I guess I haven't seen one of those commercials for a long time."

"I tell you, it's a shame. Old Style had been brewed here since around 1900, although the actual brewery had been in operation since the mid 1800's. I heard that a private equity firm bought G. Heileman in 1994 and then they sold it to Stroh's. And my local beverage distributor told me that the Old Style label has been the property of Pabst, ever since Stroh's was split between Pabst and the Miller Brewing Company."

"I never would have known," replied Michael.

"We get our fair share of customers in here from Chicago. They often order an Old Style. They say it was the official beer of the Cubs from the 1950's to just a few years back. I tell them the same thing I told you: 'I have no idea where they're brewing Old Style.' At least the old Heileman facility is back in operation, but it's now a custom brewery called City Brewery."

"What's that – a custom brewery?" asked Michael.

"That's one where they contract to brew beer for other breweries. The work force, however, at City Brewery is much smaller than when Old Style was going full speed.

"You still want an Old Style even though it's been brewed elsewhere? They're probably using the same formula."

"Sure, I'll still have one. By the way, is there much traffic along this stretch of the river?" asked Michael.

"Just keep looking out of the window and you'll be able to answer your own question. I'll get your beer and tell Carol to put your burger on the grill."

"Thanks."

The bartender walked over to the saloon style swinging doors separating the bar from the kitchen and placed Michael's order with the chef. Then he reached beneath the far end of the bar and pulled out a twelve-ounce bottle of Old Style, ambled back to Michael and placed it in front of him.

"Need a glass?" he asked.

"No. The bottle is fine," answered Michael.

"I'm Bill Snyder," said the bartender as he reached out to shake Michael's hand.

"Michael Lattimore," Michael replied.

"Here comes some now," said Bill as he glanced out the large window.

"Here comes what?" asked Michael.

"River traffic. Give it a couple of minutes and it will pass right in front of us."

Sure enough, a brigade of barges was emerging from upstream and traveling at what seemed to be a snail's pace to the south. For folks living close to the Mississippi, this was a common sight. But having grown up close to Lake Michigan and now living on the outskirts of Green Bay, seeing this kind of river traffic was a treat for Michael.

Michael informed Bill: "This is a new experience for me. As a youngster I often watched the carferries pull in and out of the harbor in Manitowoc. The carferries were taking on rail cars that they would transport across the lake. But first, the rail cars that had been brought over from the Michigan side had to be unloaded."

"What were the rail cars hauling?" asked Bill.

"Everything from grain to automobiles. The grain was going east, and the automobiles were being transported west. It was shorter going across the lake than around the lake. Carferries had been a mode of transportation since the 1890's. They operated for about one hundred years until the railroads went out; and when the trains left, so did the carferries. Every day during my childhood and youth about six carferries steamed in and out of both Manitowoc and Kewaunee on the Wisconsin side of the lake. They traveled to Ludington and Frankfort on the Michigan side."

*Angels in Disguise*

"I heard there's still one carferry operating. Am I correct?" asked Bill.

"You're right. There's still one that crosses the lake: 'The Badger.' No longer does it carry rail cars, but passengers who desire a cross-lake cruise. The boat also transports buses, trucks – even big semis – automobiles, motorcycles and bicycles. It has a limited schedule. I think it operates from sometime in May to October." In the peak season, it makes two back and forth crossings each day.

"Just how big were those carferries?" asked Bill.

Michael answered: "I don't know how long the earlier ones were, but I do know that the Badger is just over 400 feet. It was built in the early 1950's."

Michael continued: "Actually, today has been the first time I've been able to see the Mississippi River up close and personal. It's fascinating."

Bill could tell that Michael was excited about his new opportunity. "I'm glad we decided to install that large picture window a number of years ago," Bill said as he stepped away to attend to the other two patrons sitting at the bar.

Bill mixed each of them another Old Fashioned. Michael said to himself: "Evidently Old Fashioneds are as popular here as they are back home." Then Bill returned to Michael just as the set of barges, jockeyed by a tugboat, came into full view.

"What do you think they're hauling?" inquired Michael.

"Probably grain that they loaded in the Twin Cities. I gotta admit -- I never get tired of the sight," responded Bill.

"So, you're from Manitowoc?" asked Bill.

"Originally. Now we live on the far east side of Green Bay."

"Don't worry, this is a Packers bar. Most of us around here are Packers fans, even though we are located closer to the Twin Cities than we are to Green Bay," replied Bill.

"I guessed that," said Michael as he looked again at all the Green Bay Packers items on display throughout the room.

"I still consider the Vikings the 'expansion team of the early 60's,' although I must say that they've been a thorn in the Packers side since day one. Sometimes I think that instead of being called the Vikings, since they represent the Twin Cities whose baseball team is the 'Twins,' they should be the 'Twinkies' – you know.... a matching pair of soft cakes with a creamy center."

"That's a good one," Michael guffawed. "Mind if I tell that one to the folks back home in Green Bay?"

"Not at all. So, what brings you this way, Michael?"

"I'm on a two-week drive to some of the dairy farm regions of the state. I lived in Ohio for about thirty years and when I came back to Wisconsin a few years ago, I was dumbfounded by all the changes I noticed in the rural culture. So, I'm attempting to learn about these changes and how they are impacting dairy farmers and their families."

"Are you doing this for the state Ag department?" asked Bill.

"No; I'm just satisfying my own curiosity," replied Michael.

"What do you do over in Green Bay so that you can take off

on a venture like this?"

"Well, I teach. I'm a middle school social studies teacher in the Green Bay School district. I was fortunate to receive a grant from the Jefferson Foundation. This enabled me to do this summer sabbatical. Annually, the Jefferson Foundation awards about one hundred of these grants nation-wide to middle school, junior high, and high school teachers with at least twenty-five years of teaching experience."

"So, you're on a sabbatical?"

"Exactly; and the good thing is the grant covers all my expenses. I do, however, need to forward a report to them by September 15th. But I'm actually writing some pretty extensive notes each day, so composing a report should be no problem," said Michael.

"Well, I think I should probably tell you that I haven't been tending bar all my life," said Bill.

"I grew up on a dairy farm about five miles south of here. You went right past it if you drove up Highway 35. My mother passed away when she was fairly young – she was only 55 -- and when Dad retired, although most farmers I know don't really retire and Dad was one of these – he sold us the farm. We worked out a deal where we only had to pay him $1,000 a month. It was his idea. For us, it was very good deal at the time. I think he just wanted to make sure that the farm stayed in the family. It was his Dad – my Grandpa Harold, who bought it from the original owners. Dad lived with Carol and me a few years, but when his arthritis got bad – really bad – he moved into assisted living. He died five years ago.

"My two brothers wanted nothing to do with farming. They had other interests and they must have known what was ahead for too many of us dairy farmers. Carol and I did OK for a while. Oh, by the way, that's Carol back in the kitchen getting your burger ready," Bill said, as he noticed her looking out from the kitchen doorway and waving to him.

Bill went on with his story: "We even bought another 80 acres for additional crop land as our herd expanded. But then came the drought in '88, and it just devastated us. We didn't want to go any further in debt, especially after buying that neighboring 80, so we decided to sell out – cattle, machinery and the land. All except the house, a garage and an acre surrounding the house.

"Luckily, a guy from Chicago always dreamed of establishing a horse farm. He wanted to board horses and to set up a riding stable. He noticed our 'For Sale' sign while driving up 35. I've got, or I should say, had about thirty acres in woodland where he wanted to put in bridle trails. And with the view of the river as a backdrop, he thought he'd attract plenty of boarders and riders."

Michael chimed in: "Come to think of it, I do remember noticing the stable on the way up."

Bill had more to add: "Looking back now, I sometimes wish we would have kept the land or at least more than one acre. You know how much good crop land is going for these days? Thousands.

"Anyhow, like I said, he bought the land, the barn, and the outbuildings. The cattle and most of the machinery were auctioned off. I'm glad we still own the house, a two-car garage and the acre that the house is on.

"Meanwhile, Tom, my younger brother, who, a few years earlier had bought this place and the motel next door, said to

Carol and me: 'Why don't you two come and join Jackie and me at the Riverview? It's a lot of work for just the two of us. One of you could operate the bar and the other could be the chief chef.'"

Michael interjected: "It must have been Tom next door who checked me in. There's a family resemblance."

Bill nodded in affirmation and then continued his story: "Anyhow, Carol immediately thought it was a good idea. I wasn't real keen on it at first. Then Carol said: 'We've got to do something. We just can't sit around here bemoaning the sale of the farm all day long. And you know how much I like to cook. You just need to learn how to mix drinks.' Truth is, back then about the only drinks I could mix were whiskey sours, gin and tonics and screwdrivers. I didn't even know what went into an Old Fashioned – arguably the state's most requested mixed drink. So here we are, all these years later. Who'd have thought?

"I assumed the hours would be better than farming which often meant twenty-hour days, especially during harvesting season. Well, this isn't much better. We arrive here at about 10 A.M. for our 11 A.M. opening, and I don't leave until after bar time. Carol usually goes home by about 10 P.M. since we close down the kitchen at 9. Thankfully we're closed on Mondays.

"I'll be right back. I just want to check on George and Kate over there."

Bill went to the far end of the bar. A second later he reached under the bar and secured a couple of menus and offered them to his guests. Michael assumed they were "regulars" since they politely refused the menus. Plus, it wouldn't be long before Carol closed up the kitchen.

George and Kate evidently placed their order with Bill, because a moment later Bill was saying something to Carol as he was standing again at the saloon style doors leading to the kitchen. Then Bill made his way back to Michael.

"Do you miss it? The farming?" asked Michael.

"I miss it every day. Well, at least for the first couple of years. It was really rough. Guess I was going through some kind of withdrawal. Oh, there were challenges and plenty of them on the farm, don't get me wrong. And certainly, the drought presented an insurmountable one for us. But yes, I still miss it. There's nothing like newly turned soil in the early spring, or fresh cut hay that happens three or four times in late spring and summer – can't beat those smells. I miss the putt-putt sound of my John Deere. I miss the warmth of the cattle in the barn on a cold winter day. And I miss the satisfaction of seeing a ripened crop ready for harvest. I miss my girls, even though they had to be milked twice a day. You get attached to them; you know? But more than anything else, I miss the feeling of being connected to the earth. It's hard to explain unless you've been there. I believe farming keeps you 'grounded' in more ways than one."

As Bill was rattling on, Michael found himself growing nostalgic. Bill's words caused Michael to tap into his memory bank, reminding him of some of the sights, sounds and smells of his own childhood – things that Michael, too, missed. Although Michael had been raised in the country, he had not lived on a dairy farm. His childhood home, however, had been surrounded by dairy farms, and so he knew what Bill was talking about.

"Michael, are you still with me?" Bill asked, noticing a faraway look in Michael's eyes.

"Yes, I'm still listening Bill; but what you're saying takes me back to my childhood days; it's bringing back a lot of pleasant memories."

"Why's that? Were you a farm kid?"

"No. But I did grow up in the country and we were surrounded by dairy farms -- one on each side of us and another just across the road -- so I understand what you're saying. All the neighbors had John Deere's, and I do miss their unique sound. And I even miss helping them with their hay crops. But one thing I don't miss: picking stones each spring."

"You mean to tell me that spring thaw heaved up stones on the eastern side of the state?" Bill asked in jest.

"Yes, plenty."

Michael paused and then continued: "It sounds to me like you really miss farming, Bill."

"Well, like I said, I missed it terribly the first couple of years; especially when we'd pull in the driveway, see the barn and realize my girls were not coming in for milking. But eventually I think I got over it."

"Would you ever go back?" asked Michael.

"Back where?"

"To dairy farming."

"No; even if I wanted to, there's no way we could afford it," replied Bill.

"Oh, I see Carol's got your burger ready."

Bill walked over to the large rectangular hole that had been cut out of the wall between the bar and the kitchen. Framed in 1" x 4" pine boards, the bottom of the opening supported a 48" x 12" x 2" black granite counter-top which worked well as the serving counter. That's where Bill retrieved Michael's steaming hamburger loaded with grilled onions, a slice of tomato and an ample supply of lettuce; then Bill reached for a bottle of ketchup and another of mustard. As he placed the burger and condiments in front of Michael, Bill asked: "Another Old Style? This one's on the house."

Michael responded: "How about I switch to a Hamm's? That's brewed nearby, isn't it?"

"Sorry to say -- it's nearly the same story as Old Style. Hamm's used to be brewed in the Twin Cities. But not anymore. They were bought out by Stroh's and just like Old Style, I have no idea who is making the Hamm's label now. I'll bring you a can."

Bill left to retrieve a Hamm's from the cooler, and Michael -- after pouring on an ample amount of ketchup and mustard on his burger -- took his first bite. "Wonderful," he said to himself. "Good old Wisconsin bar food."

Bill returned with a can of Hamm's and a chilled glass.

"How's the burger, Buddy?" asked Bill.

"Great. Tell Carol she deserves a blue ribbon."

Realizing that Bill and he were about the same, Michael said: "Remember those Hamm's television ads from our younger days. They were pretty clever. I doubt if I'll ever forget that cartoon character bear dancing to that Native American drumbeat, and that catchy tune: 'From the land of sky-blue waters.' And I always liked how the jingle ended: 'Hamm's the beer refreshing; Hamm's the beer refreshing.' And then, in most taverns there was that iconic Hamm's motion sign that featured a scene with a waterfall and a river. Remember how the water appeared to be flowing. Those signs were a perfect complement to the lyrics of their song: 'From the land of sky-blue waters.'"

"Oh, you mean like that," said Bill pointing to a vintage Hamm's sign -- with the waterfall, flowing water and campfire -- hanging on the opposite wall. Located on the same wall as the entrance door, Michael had not noticed the Hamm's sign among the wildlife mounts and all the Packers items.

"Yes, just like that one." said Michael.

"Michael, I better let you eat your burger before it gets cold." And with that, Bill turned to tidy up the already tidy bar.

Michael didn't realize how hungry he was. He wolfed down his burger and nearly chugged his beer. As Bill returned to retrieve Michael's empty plate and hand him his tab, Michael said: "You know, we've been talking about all the changes in the beer industry: the mergers, the buyouts, and so on. But there's another change: micro-breweries. A lot of the towns I've been passing through have one. They're often a part of a restaurant or supper club. It's kind of like a hundred or more years ago when nearly every town had its own brewery. So yes, the industry has changed; but in some ways it's seems to be repeating itself with these small local breweries."

"That's an interesting observation, Michael. Maybe Carol and I should start brewing in the back room."

Then Michael reached into his wallet, pulled out three five-dollar bills, handed them to Bill, and said: "Again, my compliments to the chef."

As Bill headed toward the cash register, Michael noticed that the main door to the bar was being opened.

Bill rang up the charges and returned to Michael with his change. "Keep it," Michael said.

"I see you've got some folks you need to take care of, so I better let you go."

"O them. They come in a couple of times a week. They have a couple beers while they play cards, and then they head for home by 10 or 11."

Then Michael told Bill: "It was nice meeting you and thanks for the good conversation."

"Michael, it was good visiting. Take care and safe travels," replied Bill.

"Thank you."

With their farewells said, Michael stepped around the group heading for one of the tables and returned to his motel room. He still had to call Elaine to check on how her day went. He also wanted to fill her in on his day's activities, and then record the events and conversations that had made for a very interesting day.

It was nearly midnight when Michael turned off his light and called it a day.

# Wednesday Morning

Michel awakened at 8 A.M. He had slept well and was ready to tackle the day ahead. He showered, got dressed, and as he was tying his shoelaces a memory flashed through his mind: "Back in college I had a pair of sneakers I called my 'Go-Fasters.' On each of them was a small rubber label with the name 'Lacrosse.' I wonder if they were made here?"

He walked to the motel lobby where he ate a piece of toast and a hard-boiled egg from the breakfast bar. After he finished off a glass of orange juice, he went up to the desk to check out.

"You must be Tom," said Michael to the fella who had checked him in the previous evening.

"And you must have been talking to my brother, Bill."

"Yeah, after checking in last night I went next door and had a wonderful burger and a good conversation with Bill. We talked about some of the things going on in farming, how he and Carol left the farm to join you and Jackie in your Riverview venture. We even discussed the changes in the beer industry."

"Sounds like Bill; he'll 'talk your leg off' if you let him."

"Well, I enjoyed it and I learned a lot from our conversation. But now, I've got to ask you about something," said Michael.

"Sure, what's that?" Tom replied.

"Shoes."

"Shoes? What about them?"

"Years ago, I had a pair of gym shoes. I called them my 'Go-Fasters,' because I was convinced that I could run faster in them than any other kind of sneaker. This was back in the days before the popularity of Nike, New Balance, Saucony, and all the other brands of running shoes that have flooded the market. Anyhow, on the outside of my 'Go-Fasters' – at the back of both heals -- was a label that read: 'Lacrosse.' I'm wondering if they were made here."

Tom hesitated only a moment and then said: "I'll bet they were made here; probably at a place that was known as the Lacrosse Rubber Mill. I remember that as kids we all wore high top sneakers made by them. They were made of canvass and rubber. Boy did they stink when they got wet. You could always recognize the Lacrosse brand because there was a silhouette of a Native American embossed on the outside of each shoe – right by where your ankle bone would be. That Native American was the Lacrosse company's logo at the time."

"Are they still in business?" Michael inquired.

"Yes; but not here in Lacrosse anymore. Sometime back the Lacrosse Shoe Company – that's their more recent name – bought out the Danner Boot Company of Portland, Oregon. And not long after that they moved their office and all of their production out there – to Oregon. I don't think they make sneakers anymore, but they're known for their work boots, fire boots, hiking boots, and even fishing waders.

"Our other brother, Chet, worked for them. Started right after his discharge from the Army after serving a tour in Vietnam. He began on their production line and worked his way up to a foreman's position. When the plant closed here in Lacrosse, rather than taking an early retirement, he and Diane went out to the Pacific Northwest. And they've stayed there after retiring. They never had children and they said to Bill and me before they moved for Oregon: 'There's nothing tying us down here. This could be a new adventure for us.' They seem to like it out there. They like the outdoors and evidently they spend a lot of time in the nearby mountains. Jackie and I have gotten out there – I think three times -- since they moved. I've always come back home saying: 'It's a nice place to visit, but I wouldn't want to live there.'

"Why's that?" asked Michael.

"I'd just miss this river way too much. It's something I would wake up to every morning when I was still on the farm; and it's something we can see from our apartment above the office."

"I truly understand, "replied Michael. "The longer Elaine, my wife, and I lived in Ohio, the more I missed Lake Michigan. I was glad when we were able to move back."

"Yeah, I noticed from your registration that you're from that area."

"We live on the far east edge of Green Bay, but I grew up in Manitowoc County. As I kid I could see the lake from my upstairs bedroom window. Now we live on a ridge. By looking northwest, we can see the waters of the Green Bay."

"I understand why you would miss the lake. We've been over that way a few times and the lake shore area is beautiful – almost as scenic as this river valley."

"Well, I better get on the road. Nice to chat," said Michael. "And thanks for the information regarding my old running shoes. Come to think of it, I was wearing those shoes the night I met Elaine – my spouse," said Michael.

"I'd say those were some special shoes. Well, safe travels. Looks like it will be a nice day out there."

"So long, then," said Michael.

Michael stepped outside and headed toward his red pickup. Michael's goal for the day was to drive to Colby. Located near the very center of the state, the drive would be about 125 miles. As he had done since the beginning of his journey a week earlier, he would avoid using superhighways as much as possible and proceed along the less traveled state highways and county highways and so, after a few unavoidable miles of traveling east on Interstate 90, his plan was to proceed toward his destination via State Highways 108 and 54 to Black River Falls. Just east of Black River Falls he would turn north onto County Highways K and J and follow them to the intersection of State Highway 95. This road would take him to Neillsville where it joined state Highway 73. He'd follow it north to Highway 98 and turn east. After about a dozen miles he'd reach the village of Spencer where he'd meet State Highway 13. Then he'd turn north on 13 and only have to go another dozen or so miles to Colby. This proposed route contained many road changes, but it allowed him to see a lot of rural countryside. And again, he would make as many stops he felt were necessary.

Soon Michael was a few miles east of Lacrosse. "Changes. Changes," Michael said to himself as he looked through his rear-view mirror and watched the city of Lacrosse fading into the distance. "The changes are not only in dairy farming; but they're certainly all over the place: the beer industry, and in the transportation industry. Certainly, there's a greater reliance on trucking, and less being transported by rail or boat, he thought as his eyes scanned across the median where he noticed several large trucks heading toward Lacrosse. And changes involved with the manufacturing of footwear -- shoes and boots.

"Yes, the shoe industry," Michael mumbled to himself as he remembered that several towns in south-eastern Wisconsin – not that long ago it seemed -- had shoe manufacturers. Now only one remained. Then he thought of another industry. Several towns on the lake shore had factories that manufactured aluminum products. Many of these facilities had also closed in the past decade or two. He thought of Manitowoc, his hometown. It had been the location of the Mirro Aluminum Company – a manufacturer of aluminum cookware for over a century. At one time it had more than 3,400 employees. But not now. Its main plant had shut down several years ago and now it, and many of its smaller facilities had been razed. Michael assumed that both of these industries – shoes and aluminum cookware -- were victims of cheaper labor markets in other countries where these items could be made at a fraction of the cost of manufacturing them in the United States.

And while his mind lingered on the lakeshore, he thought about the commercial fishing industry. It too, had once thrived with fishermen harvesting loads of whitefish, lake trout and chubs. But over-fishing and sea lampreys – an invasive species originating in the north Atlantic Ocean -- caused the lake trout numbers to plummet, and many commercial fishing operations went out of business. Thankfully – in the 1970's – various strains of salmon and trout were introduced to a number of streams that flowed into the lake. Their presence has made for a successful charter fishing industry.

Then he considered a positive change: Yesterday, as he was driving from Platteville to Prairie du Chien and on to Lacrosse, he drove alongside the Mississippi River. En route he saw eagles; not just one, but well over a dozen. He remembered that as a kid and up to the late 70's bald eagles were nearly extinct. With the use of DDT as a pesticide for certain agricultural crops, it would often run off the fields and work its way into lakes and streams. There the DDT would by ingested by various fish. And when these fish were eaten by predators including bald eagles and ospreys, the DDT would enter their systems, causing a thinning of the birds' eggshells. The eggshells would then collapse under the weight off the parent incubating them. This led to a near extinction of these magnificent birds. Thankfully, banning the use of DDT has allowed bald eagles and other bird species to make a significant comeback. "Another change," said Michael, "but this time, a good one."

The next hour and a half flew by as Michael went from road to road on his way toward Colby. He noticed a number of fields with chopped hay. Michael assumed it was the second cutting of the season, and that the farmers were waiting for it to dry before it was baled.

# Late Wednesday Morning

As Michael went over a small rise in the highway, he noticed a patch of late morning fog hovering over the ground about a mile or so ahead of him. The front windows of his pickup were open and seconds later he sensed a hint of smoke. "That's not fog up ahead," he said to himself, "that's smoke."

As he drew closer he felt a sudden chill. It was not from the morning's cool breezes, but from what he knew almost instinctively. As he proceeded another ¾ mile, his suspicions were confirmed: "Barn fire. It must have happened sometime yesterday or maybe the night before, if I were to guess," said Michael to himself. Approaching the scene, he noticed the charred crumpled metal and smoldering beams that were once a part of the structure. Two dark blue Harvestore silos remained intact. The farmhouse, located close to the highway, appeared untouched by the conflagration. Several outbuildings were not affected by the blaze. "That's good," said Michael. "I hope the cows were saved." Michael was optimistic about their fate, for he did not smell any lingering stench associated with burning livestock.

Then Michael entertained a more positive thought: "Could this just have been a barn that was no longer being used?" Michael had already driven past hundreds of such barns in eight days of travel. But then he saw a collection of machinery scattered in the yard. It must have been rescued from nearby buildings – especially if those buildings had been threatened by the blaze. And after noticing a partially filled manure pit, he knew it was an active dairy farm and a barn that had been in use.

Upon passing the scene, he began to reflect on his growing up years in Manitowoc County. He remembered one summer that was particularly humid. It seemed that a barn fire was a weekly occurrence. In his mind he remembered those nights when he had seen a red glow hovering in the sky over the location of a barn fire. Why so many fires folks asked? Many blamed internal combustion – a result of putting the hay inside while it was still too moist; others said faulty wiring was the cause of the fires; and with so many occurring, many began to think that an arsonist was at work. However, after the fires had been investigated, most of the fires were recorded as "cause unknown." Now Michael wondered what may have caused the barn fire he had just passed.

A moment later he noticed his fuel gauge was indicating that his tank was only ¼ full. He wasn't surprised. Michael had not stopped for gas since he had been in Platteville three days ago. "I'm only about five miles from Neillsville. I'll get fuel there," Michael reasoned.

Just outside of Neillsville he came upon a convenience store with eight gas pumps. He pulled in the nearest bay. A sticker on the pump indicated that the fuel Michael was pumping contained 10% ethanol. While filling his tank, Michael thought to himself: "That's another change affecting agriculture. Less dependence on fossil fuels and greater use of renewable resources -- like corn. He wondered how many thousands of acres were now planted in corn to be used for ethanol -- land that had previously been pastureland or had been planted with a different crop.

Thinking of all the corn fields he had seen in the past week, Michael considered another change. He recalled a saying that had been long associated with a corn crop: "Knee high come the fourth of July." The phrase indicated the expected height of field corn at this time of the year was to reach our knees. But then, he realized that most of the corn fields he had been passing during his travels the past several days contained a corn crop that was shoulder high. This did not surprise him.

Corn stalks had been shoulder high or higher by the "fourth," for the past several years. "Yes, another change from years ago," he said to himself.

After filling his gas tank, Michael decided to enter the convenience store for a snack. So, after securing the pump's handle and hose to their proper places and gathering his receipt, he moved his truck to one of the convenience store's parking spaces just outside the front door. He was ready for a doughnut or two and a bottle of Dr. Pepper.

Michael walked in the store and as he retrieved his items and moved toward the counter to make his purchase, he noticed three fellas sitting at one of the three booths located by the store's large front window. As Michael walked past them, he heard one of them saying: "Thankfully, Herman was insured. He should be able to rebuild." Michael sensed they were discussing the barn fire that he had passed five miles back down the highway. Inquisitive as he admitted being – although Elaine called him nosy – he paid for his late morning snack and decided to take a seat in a booth immediately behind the three fellas. As he sat down, he laid his two donuts on a napkin and untwisted the plastic cap of his Dr. Pepper. Then he began to listen to their conversation. Two of the three men were facing Michael, while the third – the youngest – had his back toward Michael. Michael noticed that the oldest was wearing a long sleeve work shirt with a patch over his pocket identifying him as Willard.

"Do they know what caused it?" the youngest of the three asked.

"Some folks are saying it was probably electrical, bad wiring," said one of the fellas facing his younger companion. "After all," he continued, "the barn was at least 70 or 80 years old, and I know for a fact it had no upgrades to its electrical system."

Then Willard spoke: "No. It was fireworks. Herman had bought some cherry bombs, bottle rockets, and a whole slew of fire-crackers from that tent that's been set up over there." As he spoke he pointed out the window and across the road to a tent that appeared to be about 16'x16.' Its proprietors had just climbed out of an older van and were opening the tent flap. Their action revealed several tables filled with all sorts of ignitable and explosive stuff.

Meanwhile, Willard continued: "Herman assumed he and his boys were going to set them off on the 4th, but his boys evidently couldn't wait. Why they went out to the barn with them.... only they could tell you. But I suppose they weren't supposed to have them, and they probably thought they wouldn't be seen if they lit them in the barn. Anyhow, from what I heard from Willis Kratz, one of the bottle rockets shot deep into some old hay, igniting it. Since they were busy lighting more firecrackers, the boys didn't hear the crackling sound of the hay as it began to burn. When they finally noticed, it was too late. The fire just took off."

"Did I hear correctly that all his cattle were out in the pasture at the time of the fire?" asked the youngest of the three.

Willard responded: "Yes, thankfully, Herman and his boys had finished milking a couple hours earlier and the cows were far enough away from the barn. They did lose a lot of hay. Some from last year; almost all of this year's first crop and some of the second."

"So where are Herman's cows now?" asked the youngest.

Willard replied: "Gregg Little's got them over at his place."

Didn't Gregg sell his herd earlier this spring," asked the fella sitting next to Willard.

"He did, so he's got plenty of pastureland and his milking parlor is still fully functional. As soon as he heard that Herman had lost his barn, he called him and offered to pasture his cows and to use his barn and all his milking equipment. Gregg said that Herman could use them as long as he needed to; so Herman took him up on the offer. I heard that he told Gregg how grateful he was and then asked, 'How can I ever repay you?' Evidently Gregg just looked at him and said: 'No need to repay. It'll just be nice to have some cattle around again.'"

"'Well, let me at least pay for all the electricity I'll be using,' said Herman; and evidently Gregg was OK with that."

"Didn't Gregg lose a barn about fifteen ago?" asked the youngest.

"He did. And when he rebuilt, he put in that nice milking parlor," replied Willard. "I remember, because our son Stuart was still in high school. Stuart said: 'That's what we need, Dad.' If he only knew the cost. Well, having experienced a barn fire, it must have motivated Gregg to help someone out who's experiencing the same loss."

"You're probably right. But I'd like to think we'd all be as generous and help out in any way we could," said the youngest of the three.

By now, Michael had finished his first doughnut and about half of his Dr. Pepper. As he reached for his second chocolate covered doughnut, the conversation at the next table continued: "You know, Ron and Sam, some time ago I read that at least one in four farmers will lose a barn to fire at some point in their farming years. I don't recall exactly where I saw the article, but I'm not at all surprised by the statistic," said Willard.

"That estimate of ¼ of us losing a barn may even be a little on the low side,'" responded the fella Michael assumed was Ron.

Michael felt he had eavesdropped enough. He shoved the rest of his doughnut into his mouth, secured the cap on his half-full Dr. Pepper bottle and gave the fellas in the booth in front of him a friendly nod. The two facing him returned the gesture and Michael headed out the door. As he made his way toward his pickup, Michael considered the three fellas and their conversation. He concluded he had just been given another window into the dairy farming culture as he said to himself: "Yes, although farmers tend to be pretty independent, whenever there is a crisis, they don't hesitate to help each other out."

After he fastened his seat belt and started his engine, he paused to think: "Thankfully the cattle escaped the fire." And then he was struck with yet another realization: "With all the things dairy farmers have to worry about: bad weather, stagnant milk prices, crop failures, equipment breakdowns -- there's another constant underlying concern: fire."

With both his gas tank filled and his stomach satisfied, it was time for Michael to continue his journey toward Colby.

As Michael was driving through downtown Neillsville, his cell phone rang. He looked at the display and saw that it was Elaine.

He immediately answered and asked: "Is everything OK?"

"More than OK," Elaine responded. "Things couldn't be better. Simon and Ali are going to have a baby. We're going to be grandma and grandpa!"

It took a moment for Michael to catch his breath and when

he did, he responded: "That's wonderful news. When's the baby due?"

"Well, Ali thinks she's about two months along."

"That would make it around the end of January or the first of February." Then he added: "As soon as I get home we'll have to buy some baby clothes, unless you want to go shopping before I get there."

"I figured you'd say that. I can wait to you get home," Elaine said. "I better let you go since I know you're on the road, and I don't like talking to you on the phone when you're driving."

"I call you as soon as I get settled in somewhere for the night," Michael replied.

"I'm looking forward to it."

"Bye, grandma," teased Michael.

"I do like the sound of that." said Elaine. "Bye grandpa."

They both hung up and Michael knew that he was grinning from ear to ear.

# Early Wednesday Afternoon

About an hour later Michael was eight miles south of Colby on Highway 13. "Hey, an auction," he said to himself when he began noticing the brightly colored flags with "Dan's Auction Service" imprinted on them. Then he considered: "If it's not too far off the highway, maybe I should stop and check it out. I haven't been to a farm auction in decades."

Another two miles up the highway he came upon the site of the auction. As he pulled off to the side of the road, his pickup joined about thirty others. Many were towing cattle trailers. "A cattle auction," Michael correctly assumed.

All the action appeared to be coming from the barn. He ambled over to the large barn door which had been slid open. He heard the auctioneer "barking" from a large, cleared area that at one time housed hundreds of hay bales. As Michael's eyes adjusted to the relative darkness of the barn's interior, he saw about 35 folks sitting on folding chairs. A closer look indicated that the group was all men, and most were dressed in overalls. Almost all of them were holding bidding cards.

From a nearby table Michael secured a brochure that indicated 60 Holsteins cows were being auctioned. The front of the brochure featured a colored photo of an almost all black Holstein and underneath was the name "Daisy Mae." Michael walked over to a fella who had just entered the barn and asked: "What's this all about?" pointing to the picture of Daisy Mae.

The fella immediately told Michael: "That's Daisy Mae. She has been Sid's favorite ever since she was born. She was a breech birth, and it was a miracle that she survived. See that patch of white on her forehead. Sid said it looked like a daisy and since she was born in May, Sid named her Daisy Mae. He names all his cows; or maybe I should say 'named' all his cows. He says he doesn't want them to become just a number; and he says that by treating them like a member of the family, they have better milk production."

"Thank you, I was just wondering how this particular cow was chosen to have her picture on the brochure," said Michael.

"Sid said that if a picture of one of his herd was to be used for the auction brochure – it could only be Daisy Mae."

"Thank you," said Michael. "I take it that you and Sid are good friends?"

"Friends since we were kids."

"I just hope I'm not too late," said the fella as he hustled off and secured a bidder's card from the nearby folding table and then found a seat among the bidders.

"Late for what?" Michael asked; but Michael's voice had been drowned out by the racket of the auctioneer and the bidders.

Then Michael noticed another fella sitting by himself, way down at the far end of the cavernous space. A hay bale served as his chair. Michael felt compelled to go over to him.

As Michael drew closer, he noticed the man was quietly weeping. Michael's instincts told him that the man he was approaching was the dairy farmer whose herd was being auctioned. Although he was bent over and almost in a fetal position, Michael guessed him to be in his early 60's and weighing in at about a 180 pounds. As he looked up to Michael who was approaching him, Michael noticed that his face and arms were well-tanned, undoubtedly from hours on the tractor planting corn and beans and cutting and baling hay.

"You must be Sid," said Michael. "Mind if I sit a spell?"

"Not if you don't mind a blubbering old coot like me."

Sid pointed to a neighboring bale and Michael leaned over and shoved it to within a few feet of Sid and sat down.

"Hard day for you?" asked Michael.

"Terrible day."

"How long have you been milking?" asked Michael.

Sid looked up and replied: "After today, it's not have been, but had been. But to answer your question: A long time – probably since I was about eight or nine years old. I can remember helping my grandpa in this very barn. Then I milked with Dad. And for about the last twenty-five years, it's been me and my boy -- when he was still home."

"That's been a good while." said Michael.

"Grandpa and Dad made it through rough times. They must be looking down today, shaking their heads and saying: 'What a failure!'"

Hearing Sid's comment, Michael's mind immediately transported him back to Sunday at St. Joe's Church where Father Francis, during his homily, had said: "Just because something we attempt fails, that doesn't make us failures; for God doesn't call us to be successful, he calls us to be faithful. Our ultimate value is not found in what we do, but rather, our value comes from who we are an to whom we belong. And who are we?" asked Fr. Francis. He paused a few seconds before he continued: "We are children of a loving and forgiving God. That's what gives us value, no matter if we are successful at what we do or not."

Michael was pulled back from his daydreaming when Sid went on: "See that rope hanging on that hook over there? Lately I feel like I should hang it from the rafters, tie a noose around it, put it around my neck and jump. Then my troubles would be over."

Michael, being a complete stranger, was surprised by Sid's straight-forward revelation. At the same time, he was pleased that Sid was so candid with him. Michael knew he had to reply: "Sid, is it really that bad?" probed Michael.

"I can't think of anything worse... other than losing Janice."

"Well, can I tell you some good news, Sid?" asked Michael.

"I could sure use some."

"I'm going to be a grandpa – for the first time. Just found out about an hour ago as I was driving through Neillsville."

"Good news for you. But how is that good news for me?" questioned Sid.

"Well hold on Sid," said Michael. "I'm going somewhere with this. Sid, do you have grandchildren?"

"Yes, six of them."

"Good. And do you remember your grandpa?"

"Yes, of course I do."

"Well tell me then, what are your favorite memories of him?"

inquired Michael.

"Well, give me a second," said Sid as he reached up to scratch his head. "I already told you about milking with him. He taught me how to fish down at the creek. And he let me the drive the tractor before Dad would let me. That remained our special little secret until the first time Dad was going to let me drive. As Dad was trying to show me how to brake and shift gears on the John Deere, I interrupted him and said, 'I already know how to do that.' Then Dad asked: 'How's that?' I had a one-word answer: 'Grandpa.' Dad let out a howl and said: 'I should have figured as much.'"

"So, let me ask you, Sid," asked Michael: "Do those good memories involve stuff – possessions – and are they about success?"

"I suppose not."

"But what makes them so special or important to you?" challenged Michael.

"Grandpa was spending time with me."

"Exactly!"

"What I'm getting at Sid, is a wonderful gift you still have: time. Time to do things with your grandchildren. That's how I hope you want them to remember you – spending time with them; doing things together and simply enjoying each other's company. And if I may be blunt: That's a far cry from a memory of you dangling from the end of a rope."

Sid let out a deep gasp that sounded like the air escaping from a balloon. He reached out toward Michael, put his arms around him, and began to sob; not quietly, but uncontrollably, with shoulders shaking and body trembling. They were tears expressing the kind of grief that had been building up for some time, and they were now flowing freely, like the water from a dam that had been dynamited. It merely took someone to push the right emotional button. And Michael was that someone.

The emotional outburst lasted for more than a minute. Then there was a moment of silence before Sid drew back from Michael, gathered his composure and said: "You're right. You're absolutely right! What makes you so darn smart?"

"It's not me, Sid. It all goes back to a discussion I had with a friend years ago. His name was John. John told me something that has stayed with me for nearly forty years. He said: 'In the end, what matters most is not the quantity of our possessions or even the number of our accomplishments, but what is most important is the quality of our relationships.' That simple but profound advice has helped me more than once over the years, especially those times whenever I started feeling like a failure."

"Well then. This John fella is one smart cookie," replied Sid. "You haven't told me your name."

"I'm Michael, Michael Lattimore."

"Glad to make your acquaintance, Michael. My last name is Roberson," said Sid.

"Hey Michael, I'm a little hungry. How 'bout we go over to the food stand that's set up by my machine shed. I'll buy you a brat?"

"That sounds good, Sid. But first, there's something I need to say to you: You just told me that you were feeling pretty desperate, even to the point of considering suicide. I take what you said seriously. And you need to take those feelings of desperation and helplessness seriously. You can get through this. But don't try to do it alone. There are others out there who are experiencing some of the same things. And there are programs designated to help you – and to get you back on your feet – emotionally. Your county Ag extension office should have information on all these programs. So, will you promise me that tomorrow you'll call the Ag office and check to see what's available for you?"

"Yes," Sid replied.

"Yes, what?" Michael insisted.

"Yes, I promise, Michael."

"OK then, let's get that brat. Got to see if they're as good as the ones from Manitowoc or Sheboygan County."

"They're pretty darn good. They're made right up the road in Abbotsford."

On the way to the food stand Sid stopped and turned toward Michael who now also stood still, and asked: "Michael, I see you're not bidding. So, what made you stop?"

"I don't know. I just felt like I needed to. Plus, I haven't been to an auction in ages."

"Well, I'm very grateful you decided to stop."

"I 'm glad I stopped, too," said Michael.

As they continued toward the food stand, they passed the auction ring just as the auctioneer announced: "We're down to thirteen head of the original sixty." Suddenly, one of the bidders called out to the auctioneer: "I'll take them all except that one that's almost all black, and I'll bid $1300 a head."

All the other bidders were stunned by this rather bold move. Then they started whispering among themselves. Meanwhile, the brash announcement from the bidder also caught the attention of Sid and Michael and they paused to watch the action.

Sid realized that the one cow the bidder didn't want was Daisy Mae, his favorite cow – the same cow Sid insisted be on the cover of the auction brochure. He told Michael that the bidder must have done his research on the cows being offered and knew that Daisy Mae's milk production was not on a par with the others.

Then Sid recognized the bidder as Adam Smith of "Adam and Eva's Dairy" – a mega farm just outside of Stratford. Sid knew exactly what Adam was doing. He said to Michael: "He was just waiting to see what all the other cows were going for; and when the bids started to drop, he offered an amount that he knew would be just a bit higher than the other bidders would offer."

"Sounds a little sneaky to me," replied Michael.

"Well, he's got to live with himself. Let's get out of here. I've seen enough," said Sid with a tone of disgust.

As Michael and Sid resumed their walk to the food stand, the auctioneer said: "I've got $1300 a head for all the rest except that nearly all black one. Do I hear $1350 a head?" Just as Sid foretold, no one raised a bidding card. "How about $1325 a head." Again, there were no bidders. The auctioneer asked the bidders once again: "$1325 a head?" Still, no one responded.

So he continued: "Going once, going twice, sold for $1300 a head – all of them except Blackie -- to Adam Smith of Adam and Eva's Dairy."

Sid stopped abruptly and looked at Michael and said: "Dan, the auctioneer; he should know better. Her name is not Blackie; it's Daisy Mae."

After Michael and Sid got their brats and drinks and sat down at a picnic table, Sid asked Michael: "You mentioned coming through Neillsville. You've come quite a way for an auction that you aren't even bidding at."

Michael sensed Sid was asking a question more than making an observation, so Michael decided to disclose to Sid how he ended up at Sid's farm.

Michael began: "I'm actually from Green Bay. I've been on the road for a little over a week. I've been going to the state's dairy farm regions and studying how all the changes going on are affecting dairy farmers and their families."

"Well, I guess you've come to the right place. Unfortunately, some of those changes have led some of us to become rather desperate," said Sid.

"I know," responded Michael.

"Hey Sid, I'm sorry to interrupt, but I've been looking for you."

"Hi Alfred. Let me introduce you to Michael."

"Michael, this is my neighbor and good friend, Alfred."

Michael, recognizing Alfred as the fella he had spoken with

shortly after he entered the barn, said to Sid: "We actually talked to each other a little while ago in the barn."

"Good to officially meet you," Michael said.

"I want you to know right away," Alfred said to Sid. "I bid on Daisy Mae and I got her."

Sid, looking a little dismayed and hurt that his good friend would buy his favorite animal, said to Alfred: "You what?! Why would you ever want to do that? You and I both know her milk production hasn't been up to snuff. And you said yourself a few days ago: 'My present herd is all that I can handle.'"

"Sid, I bought her so I could give her back to you."

"What?" Sid said in amazement. "You can't do that."

"I know how much Daisy Mae means to you – really, to us. I'll never forget the night you called over to our house. Dr. Vittle was gone. You needed help with her birth. Bessie, her mother. was struggling to birth her. Thankfully we were able to get her out. After she was born you were about to call her Midnight, but then you said that there's a flower on her head and you decided to call her Daisy. But then you also said: 'It's May; let's call her Daisy Mae.' And I know she's been your favorite ever since."

Turning to Michael, Sid said: "I always gave our calves names. My Dad used to tell me that when you gave something a name, you took responsibility for it. Dad said that idea goes way back to Adam; that God instructed Adam to give all the animals a name, and when he did, he was assuming responsibility for them. And I'd like to think I was responsible for all the cattle we've ever owned. Speaking of Adam, I wonder if Adam Smith gives any of his cows a name? I doubt it."

"Sid," said Alfred, "I want you to have Daisy Mae. Keep her for a pet for the grand kids."

"But who's going to milk her? I can't milk just one cow."

"They did back in the old days," said Alfred.

"But you and I both know – these are not the old days. Add her to your herd, Alfred."

"No. I bought her for you."

"How much did you have to bid to get her?" inquired Sid.

"It didn't matter. I made up my mind I was getting her for you -- no matter what," responded Alfred.

"Well, I'm not about to milk just one cow. Take her. I know she'll be in good hands."

"If you insist, but you come over and visit her any time you wish."

"Thanks Alfred. You know you just did about the nicest, kindest thing anybody has ever done for me."

"That's what friends are for. I better get Daisy Mae loaded up."

"Need any helping getting her in your trailer?"

"No. You just stay here and visit with Michael. I know it's been a rough day for you."

With those empathetic words offered, Alfred turned and walked toward the temporary pen that held Daisy Mae.

"Wow," said Michael, "You're absolutely right. What a tremendous act of kindness!"

After they finished their brats, Michael felt it was time to continue on toward Colby. He said farewell to Sid.

Sid responded: "So long, Michael, and thank you for helping me to see things much more clearly."

They exchanged "good-byes" and Michael returned to his truck parked along Highway 13.

# Later Wednesday Afternoon

Michael resumed his travel and arrived in Colby within ten minutes. He drove through town, continued on for a couple of miles and located a motel near the entrance to Abbotsford – a town just north of Colby. He checked in to the Starlight Inn and called Elaine. She clicked on her phone and said: "Michael, you're calling already?"

"Just wanted to ask if there was anything new on the baby front?" he asked Elaine.

"Nothing new since we talked a few hours ago. Are you going to be calling me every couple of hours to ask about Ali's pregnancy?"

"No. But one thing I do know -- when I get home, we'll have to go over to Kohl's."

"Are you still thinking about baby clothes?" wondered Elaine.

"Of course," replied Michael.

"Well I have to admit that I've been thinking about of those cute little outfits, too."

After updating her on the day's events including his encounter with Sid, Michael listened as Elaine described in detail how her summer job of teaching remedial reading was progressing. She was especially proud of one student who she said, "was catching on." "I've got him reading some books on the Packers. That seems to have really motivated him," Elaine said with a sense of satisfaction.

After his conversation with Elaine, Michael jotted down some detailed notes regarding the day's events. It had been another full day. He was tired, but decided to get a light supper, and then come back and go to bed fairly early. But first, he wanted to give Simon and Ali a call and congratulate them on the upcoming birth. It was a little before 5 P.M. He assumed that they'd both be home. Simon was working with the summer youth recreation program in Ripon and his workday usually finished around 4 P.M. Meanwhile, Ali's work day at Jepsen Medical Supply typically also ended by 4 P.M.

"Simon," Michael said as Simon answered his cell phone. "I hear you're going to be a Daddy. That's great news."

Simon responded: "Did Mom tell you? I tried calling earlier but you must have had your phone turned off."

"I don't remember it being off and yes, before you ask, I'm trying to do better keeping it charged. Oh, I know what happened. I stopped at a convenience store for fuel and then went in for a couple of donuts and left my phone in the pickup. I bet that's when you tried calling. Is Ali feeling OK?"

"Yes, she is. We figure she's about two months along. Dad, I might need some pointers along the way. This is all new territory for me," said Simon.

"Don't worry, Simon, you're going to be a great Dad. But know that I'm always here if you need me."

Michael and Simon chatted a while longer and then Simon said: "I'm gonna have to let you go, Dad. I'm meeting Ali at the Blue Moon Supper Club – kind of a celebratory dinner."

"You just keep treating that young woman the way you always have."

"Don't worry Dad. I'll talk to you soon."

"Good-bye Simon, I love you and give my love to Ali."

Michael clicked out of his call, made sure he had his truck keys, the motel key and his wallet and walked out the door. He was ready to find a place for supper.

# Early Wednesday Evening

Michael stopped at the front desk to ask: "Where's a good place for supper?"

The desk clerk gave him directions to "Mom and Pops," telling Michael that was located just off Highway 29. It was less than a mile away.

Michael assumed he was headed for a "mom and pop" family-style restaurant, but when he entered the parking lot Michael noticed that the establishment was actually called "Mom and Pop's Supper Club." He entered and took a seat at a small table. A perky waitress, appearing to be in her early 20's, approached him with a water pitcher, filled his water glass, and handed him a menu. Then she asked him: "Anything else to drink besides water? We've got all kinds of beer on tap and we're known for our Old Fashioneds."

"No thank you. Actually, I'm ready to order."

"Can I have a grilled cheese sandwich, a house salad with French and a large glass of milk?"

"Sure thing, although our rib-eyes are to die for."

"I don't doubt it. But I need to go light for supper night," responded Michael.

When the waitress asked him what kind of cheese he wanted on his sandwich, Michael did not hesitate to request Colby.

The waitress giggled a second or two and then responded: "Sorry, we don't have any Colby." Michael appeared a little disappointed. Then a big smile came over the face of the waitress and she admitted: "I'm just pulling your leg. Colby is our best seller and we always keep a good supply of it."

"You had me worried there for a second," said Michael. "I had been saying to myself: 'When in Colby, eat Colby.'"

"Do you want your milk now or with your meal?"

"Along with the sandwich and salad, please."

Since the restaurant was not busy, Michael's order arrived within a few minutes. Michael hadn't realized he was as hungry as he was, and he finished his meal very quickly.

After leaving a tip for his waitress he side-stepped over to the cash register and paid his bill. Then as he turned to exit the restaurant, he saw them in a booth in the back corner: Sid Roberson and a woman whom Michael assumed to be Janice, Sid's wife. Michael had not seen them when they had arrived at the restaurant moments earlier.

"Should I just wave and leave them alone, or should I go over to say 'Hello?'" While Michael was pondering his conundrum, Sid looked up and saw Michael. Immediately Sid motioned for Michael to come over. Michael thought: "I guess my dilemma is solved."

Upon reaching Sid's table, Sid stood and said to his companion: "Janice, this is Michael, the fella who stopped by the auction earlier. The one I told you about."

Turning to Michael, Sid continued: "Michael, this is my wife Janice. I'm a lucky man. She continues to stand with me through all the ups and downs."

Immediately Janice said to Michael: "Thank you. Thank you, Michael, for what you did for Sid earlier this afternoon. Sid told me all about it."

"I assume you're alone, Michael; why don't you join us?" asked Sid.

"Actually, I just finished and was on my way out," Michael responded.

"Well, you can still sit and chat awhile, can't you?"

"It would be my pleasure, Sid."

As Michael took a seat and joined Sid and Janice, a waitress arrived and filled their water glasses. "I'm Beverly, and I'll be taking care of you. Is anything else I can get you to drink? Our Old Fashioneds are great. We've got several beers on tap and Coke products, plus iced tea and lemonade. Oh, I almost forgot, we have a good selection of wines – born European and domestic."

Janice ordered a glass of Riesling; Sid opted for a pint of Spotted Cow beer; and Michael settled for a decaf coffee.

When Beverly left to fill their drink order, Sid announced: "Before you ask, Michael – I told Janice all about my episode earlier this afternoon, and how you got me thinking straight once again."

"I assumed that when Janice said, 'Thank you.'"

Janice spoke up: "And Sid told me what Alfred did --- buying Daisy Mae and offering her back to us. I know how much Sid is attached to Daisy Mae. I think Alfred's offer eased the pain of selling the herd a little bit. As you know, Daisy Mae is pretty special. That was a wonderful offer that Alfred made."

"It certainly was," agreed Michael.

Then Janice continued: "I never would have imagined how desperate Sid was feeling. I knew something was up, but he never wanted to talk about it. He seemed to become more withdrawn. More detached. Like he was living in a different world the last couple of months. I thought whatever was bothering him would finally pass once we decided to auction the cows. But it didn't. Still I never thought that he'd consider taking his life."

Beverly returned with their drink order. Sid, Janice and Michael suspended their conversation while Beverly asked them if they were ready to order. Janice opted for a vegetable stir-fry and Sid ordered a rib-eye accompanied by a baked potato and side salad. "Thousand Island on the salad and I'd like the steak medium-rare. I'll wait with the salad until everything else comes out," requested Sid.

Beverly turned to Michael and said, "I know you've already eaten, but can I get you anything else?"

Michael responded with a polite: "No thank you."

After the waitress left to place their order with the chef, Michael asked: "How do you feel you made out with the auction?"

"OK, I guess. I didn't really know what to expect. But at least it's over," answered Sid.

Then Michael leaned in closer to Sid and said: "Sid, I'm guessing the desperation you've been feeling didn't come on overnight; what I gather from what Janice just said is that it's probably been coming – creeping up on you for several weeks, maybe even months – like a slow-moving black cloud that finally came to rest right on top of you."

Sid interrupted: "Accurately described; but I'm like all the rest of the guys I know. Independent. Proud. Always thinking we can handle our own problems."

Michael continued: "Well Sid, just as it took quite a while to reach a boiling point, I need to remind you that the challenges you guys face and those feelings of desperation that settle in on you don't disappear overnight. Yes, today you had a critical moment and seemed to have had a breakthrough, but you don't know what tomorrow may bring. That's why I told you earlier to call the county Ag office and ask them what programs they know of that may be helpful to you and to others who are facing similar circumstances."

While Michael was speaking, he suddenly remembered something: He always carried a few cards listing the 800 number for a suicide hotline. He didn't know why he hadn't thought of this information earlier. Acutely aware of the difficult home lives of some of his students and realizing the peer pressure and the bullying that students were often subjected to, Michael knew devastating effects these forces could have upon young people. He feared that some of these pressures might cause some young people to consider suicide. So, he carried these hotline business cards "just in case" he ever suspected that a student might actually consider taking his or her life; or even if he heard that a student was just "joking around" about it. So he secured one of the cards from his wallet and reached over the table to give it to Sid.

"What's this?" asked Sid.

"It's the number for a suicide hotline."

"You really think I still need this?" asked Sid as he took the card from Michael.

"What do you think, Sid?"

Sid didn't answer Michael's question. Instead, he accepted the card from Michael, and replied: "I never asked you, Michael, are you a psychologist?"

"No. I'm a middle school social science teacher. But in all honesty, I have taken quite a few psychology courses over the years. I always want to be aware of any signs a student may be giving off that might call for some sort of intervention."

"I'm guessing that earlier today you 'read me like a book,'" said Sid.

"You could say that. Even though several folks were in your barn, you chose to be alone – away from the group, sitting there with your head down, while all the action of the auction was taking place just a few steps away. You weren't saying anything, and your posture was as if you were wearing a sign saying: 'I need help.'"

"And so, you came to my rescue."

"Just a matter of being in the right place at the right time." said Michael.

"Like a guardian angel," concluded Sid.

"I wouldn't go that far."

Then Michael had a request: "Sid, will you give me your cell phone number? I want to call you tomorrow to check in with you just to see how you are doing; and I also want to make sure you called either the Ag office or the hotline number I

*Angels in Disguise*

just gave you."

"Better yet, why don't you come over for breakfast in the morning; and you can watch me make the call. That's the least we can do. Isn't that right, Janice?"

Janice replied: "Yes, by all means; come over. You already know where we live."

Michael responded: "OK. I'll be there. What time?"

"How about eight o'clock? I don't have cows to milk, so I can sleep in. Is that OK with you Janice?"

"That's fine with me," replied Janice.

"OK. Eight o'clock it is. I better let the two of you go so you can eat in peace. I know it's been a long rough day for the two of you and you need some quiet time together," said Michael.

"Thank you for your thoughtfulness," said Janice. "We'll see you in the morning."

"Until then," responded Michael.

"Yes, until then," echoed Sid.

As Michel walked toward the main door of the restaurant, Beverly returned to Sid and Janice with their entrees. Suddenly Michael stopped and reached in his pocket for a pen and an extra napkin he had placed there earlier. Staring at a small bulletin board just inside the door, he wrote something on the napkin. Then he turned and walked out the door and to his pickup.

When he arrived back at the motel, Michael showered and

hopped into bed. He located the remote and tuned in to the Brewers game. His favorite major league team was in the midst of a three-game series with the San Francisco Giants. He must have dozed off for the next thing he knew it was midnight. He reached for the remote and turned off the TV. Sleep returned quickly.

# Thursday Morning

After getting dressed, Michael checked out of the Starlight, got back out on Highway 13 and headed for Sid and Janice's place. He arrived within twenty minutes. As soon as he stepped out of his pickup, Michael was greeted by Sid and Janice's friendly collie. As Michael walked toward the door, it was opened by Janice who said cheerfully: "Come in. Come in, Michael. Make yourself at home."

He entered the large kitchen and shook hands with Sid who was waiting by the table.

"'Come and sit down; take a load off your feet," said Sid.

In a moment, Michael and Sid were seated at the table and Janice was removing a breakfast casserole from the oven. It was baked oatmeal.

Once Janice was seated, Sid spoke: "I'm not one to pray a lot, but I think that maybe I should start. Michael, would you mind if I said a word?"

"No; not at all," said Michael; and Janice nodded in agreement.

"Lord, you know our needs. And you supply them by your goodness. Thank you for this food, for this new day and for sending Michael to us. Amen."

Sid reached for a large serving spoon, placed it in the oatmeal and then attempted to lift the casserole. He intended to pass it to Janice and Michael. But he immediately discovered it was too hot and so he announced: "How 'bout you hand me your plates and I'll dish it out?"

Michael nodded to Janice, indicating that she go first. She did;

then Sid served Michael a good-sized serving before taking some for himself.

"This is excellent," said Michael.

"'I agree," reported Sid. "Why haven't you ever made this before?"

"'I just came across the recipe and thought I'd give it a try."

"Well, you can make it any time you want," said Sid.

Their breakfast conversation centered around their families. Sid and Janice spoke of their son, Silas. "Can you believe it!" Janice exclaimed, "Silas is our only child, and he and Maria end up having six children – three of each."

Then Michael spoke about Elaine who, he said, was teaching remedial reading this summer. He spoke proudly of his daughter, Sarah, who was working in Milwaukee with a non-for-profit agency seeking to provide adequate housing for the poor and exploited; and his son, Simon, who was an elementary school teacher in Ripon. He went on to say: "And as you already know Sid, Simon and his wife Ali are expecting their first child -- our first grandchild."

Janice quickly responded: "You and Elaine will soon discover one of life's greatest blessings – grandchildren."

As they finished their first serving and while Sid was dishing out a second, Michael said: "Sid and Janice, I need to tell you about something I saw last night on the bulletin board at 'Mom and Pop's.' It caught my eye as I was leaving. Knowing I was going to see you this morning, I jotted down the information."

Michael handed Sid the white napkin from the restaurant. Sid unfolded it, revealing the note Michael had recorded.

"What's it say?" Janice eagerly asked.

Sid read: "Help needed to house and raise calves for a large dairy operation. Call Ken at 592-2020."

"I shouldn't assume anything, but I could tell yesterday how much you love livestock. I just thought, maybe..."

Sid interrupted him: "I know. You thought this is something I could do, especially after selling my cows. Maybe I'll check it out. But first, I've got another phone call to make."

"To the county Ag offices?" asked Michael.

"Yes, I promised that I would, and I keep my promises." said Sid.

Janice wondered: "It's only 8:15. Do you think they're in?"

Sid replied: "I would assume so. They deal with farmers and we're all early risers."

Sid excused himself from the table, reached for his cell phone on the kitchen counter, pulled open a cabinet drawer, and lifted out a Marathon County phone book. Then he stepped into the doorway leading from the kitchen to the living room. It seemed as if Sid wanted both Janice and Michael to hear his conversation. Then he found the number he was looking for. He punched in the number and let it ring several times. Sid remained quiet. His expression indicated he was listening intently.

Sid clicked off his phone, and both Janice and Michael asked simultaneously: "Well?"

"You were right, Janice. Got a message saying they were in meetings until 10 A.M."

Sid then reached in the pocket of his blue flannel shirt and pulled out the small card Michael had given him the previous evening at "Mom and Pops." It was the number for the suicide prevention hotline.

Sid took his position once again between the kitchen and the living room and punched in the 800 number. Janice and Michael could not hear the voice from the other end of the line, but they could hear Sid.

"Yes. I think I may need some help. We haven't been making it on the farm and we had to sell our herd. I've been farming all my life and I don't know what to do. I wake up each morning feeling as if I'm a failure. I'm kind of at a loss. Yesterday, as our herd was being auctioned, it got so bad that I talked about taking my own life."

Michael and Janice could tell that the hotline operator was now responding, because Sid did not speak for a moment. Then he said: "Yes, suicide. But thankfully a wonderful fella who stopped at the auction and who is sitting right now at our kitchen table, talked some sense into me."

Again, the hotline counselor must have been speaking for Sid was quiet. Then he responded, "I'm calling from central Wisconsin, near Colby."

There was a long lull before Sid reached for a piece of paper from the kitchen counter and began writing.

Another moment passed and then Sid replied: "Yes, I'm

feeling much more positive today. In fact, the best I've felt in a couple of months."

Again Sid the appeared to be listening intently, and then he said: "715-989-8678."

Seconds later and Sid was saying: "Yes, I will. Thank you. Goodbye."

Sid clicked off his cell phone and returned to his place at the kitchen table.

"Well Sid, what did they say?" asked Janice.

"She – a woman who identified herself as Barbara -- assured me that we're not the only ones who have had to sell their cows and give up milking; but I already knew that. She also said I am not the only one with feelings of despair and no longer feel useful. Then she gave me the numbers of both a psychologist and a psychiatrist who specialize in helping farmers and their families to cope with their unique challenges. She also gave me the number for a support group that meets in Wausau. I sensed she was reading from a listing of nearby resources, because she paused a couple of times as if she was looking something up.

"Then she said that the facilitator of the group in Wausau is a Dr. Crosby. He's the psychologist she had just mentioned. Then she told me: "It appears from my information that there are about ten farmers in the support group who either have experienced or are experiencing some of same of the same things you've been going through -- both financially and emotionally.' She said they come together twice a month, and they are supporting each other and learning how to cope with all the changes in their lives. Then, you heard me give her my cell number. She asked for it because she said either she or another phone counselor would be calling back to check on me to see what I was going to do with the information she was giving me."

Then Sid said, "Excuse me for a moment." He reached for both his phone and the small piece of paper he had written on moments earlier. Then he punched in a set of numbers. A few seconds later Sid was asking: "Can you tell me when the farmers support group meets, and exactly where?"

Sid turned over his piece of paper and wrote the information he had just been given.

And then he asked, "Should Janice, my wife, come too?"

"OK," Sid replied, "Thank you very much."

"You did it," said a smiling Michael to Sid.

"Yes Dear, I'm proud of you," echoed Janice.

"Yes, I think the support group is my first step in all of this," said Sid.

"My first step?" Janice asked, "Isn't it our first step? I can come with you, can't I?"

"You certainly can, and I am glad you want to," said Sid gratefully.

Sid and Janice quickly cleared the dishes and Janice offered Michael another cup of coffee.

"Just a half of cup, please. Thank you."

As Janice poured Michael's coffee, Sid turned to Michael and said: "I want to tell you, Michael, I had a strange dream during the night, and I think you were in it. Like I said earlier, I don't consider myself a religious man, although I do attend mass once in a while. Anyhow, last night I had a dream where there was some sort of figure standing by the entrance to the barn -- the entrance the folks used for the auction."

"What sort of figure are you talking about?" asked Janice.

"I think it was an angel. In fact, in my dream, I can remember hearing myself say: 'Wow! An angel.' Although he had kind of a shimmering appearance and a glow about him, I didn't notice any wings and he wasn't wearing a gown or robe, but a shirt – the very same kind of light blue denim shirt that you were wearing yesterday, Michael. I don't know if that makes you some kind of  angel, but you sure showed up when I needed help, and I want to thank you and the good Lord."

"You're welcome. But remember I'm just a middle school social studies teacher."

"Well," said Sid, "I just thought you needed to know."

"Janice and Sid, I need to get on my way. Thank you for your hospitality. And I hope all goes well with your support group in Wausau. I'm really glad you're going to see what it's all about."

"I'm actually looking forward to it."

"Me too," said Janice.

As Sid walked Michael to the door, Sid held out his hand and, vigorously shaking Michael's hand, said: "If you get back to this area, stop in again."

"I'd like to be able to do that. And I'd like for you to meet my wife, Elaine. Thank you again. Best wishes to you and have a good Independence Day."

"You too, Michael," said Janice.

Michael stepped out of the door, proceeded down the front steps and got into his pickup. He pulled out of Sid and Janice's driveway and back onto the highway.

As he drove toward Colby, he realized that amid all the events of yesterday afternoon and this morning, he still hadn't found the answer to a question he thought of on the previous day: "Does the village of Colby get its name from the cheese; or is Colby cheese named after this village where it was first produced?" Michael suspected the later, but he would soon check with the locals at the co-op store, if they had one, and get the definitive answer.

Meanwhile, as Sid and Janice watched Michael disappear up the highway, Janice turned to Sid and asked: "Do you really consider Michael to be an angel?"

Sid replied: "Maybe like 'an angel in disguise.' Don't you remember when Father Sulkowski gave us a lesson on the archangels? Michael was the name of one of them. Maybe it's all a coincidence; or maybe it's not. I'm just sure glad he stopped by yesterday when he did and that we had a chance to spend some time with him last night and again this morning."

Then Sid said: "Janice, I know I'm changing the subject, but what do you think about us checking into raising a bunch of calves?"

Janice replied: "I don't think it would hurt one bit. It might be exactly what the good Lord has in store for us."

www.ingramcontent.com/pod-product-compliance
Lightning Source LLC
Chambersburg PA
CBHW062040120526
44592CB00035B/1726